The Benefit
of Faith

The Benefit of Faith

Whayne R. Clarke Sr.

TATE PUBLISHING
AND ENTERPRISES, LLC

Published by Tate Publishing & Enterprises, LLC
127 E. Trade Center Terrace | Mustang, Oklahoma 73064 USA
1.888.361.9473 | www.tatepublishing.com

Tate Publishing is committed to excellence in the publishing industry. The company reflects the philosophy established by the founders, based on Psalm 68:11,
"The Lord gave the word and great was the company of those who published it."

Published in the United States of America

ISBN: 978-1-63185-792-8
1. Religion / Christian Life / Inspirational
2. Religion / Christian Life / Spiritual Growth
14.02.18

Introduction

James tells us to be doers of the word. The word is meant to produce action. Hebrews 4:12 says, "*the word that God speaks is alive and full of power making it active, operative, energizing, and effective.*" This can only happen in the believer's life when we become doers of the word. Many Christians, however, take a passive approach for example; my family was on vacation in Florida and we were getting ourselves ready for the day's activities. My wife and I were telling our daughter, who was 13 at the time, to get up and get washed and dressed so we could get on with the day. Of course she was in the middle of watching television, and Lord knows you don't mess with a teenager while they're watching television, so we had to tell her a few times. She finally replied by saying "I hear you" so I responded with "then why aren't you moving?" This is how many Christians act when God gives them a command or direction. We hear the word, but refuse to act. We make up excuses that we are tired, or, like my daughter, we're busy doing our own thing, or we are afraid displaying our true lack of faith. How does this relate to The Benefit of Faith? The word doer means maker, producer, author, or simply put, owner. We must take ownership of the word and make it ours. In order to take ownership of something we must believe in it. When we believe and act on the word, we receive the benefit of our faith. The title is taken from Hebrews 4:2.

Benefit 1

The first benefit is God will keep you. One of the greatest Old Testament examples of this is the story of Joseph [Gen 37-50]. He started out as the apple of his father's eye not knowing it would lead to a life filled with troubles. He was favored above all his brothers, and they knew it as well. He was probably the equivalent of today's spoiled brat, and his brothers did not appreciate it one bit. Joseph's dreams only fueled their rage, so they decided to get rid of him. They sought to kill him and would have succeeded if not for Reuben. Instead, they decided to sell him to the Ishmaelites for twenty pieces of silver. He was taken down to Egypt and there sold into the hand of Potiphar. However, the lord was with him and he, in spite of his situation, still prospered [Gen 39:2]. Even Potiphar recognized that God was with Joseph. Even in our worst trials, others need to know God is with us, and it is apparent that Joseph continued to follow the principles of God even in this bad situation, a lesson for us today.

Because of his character, Joseph was promoted to overseer of all that his master had. He had so much control that Potiphar himself had to consult Joseph about his own possessions, everything, except for the bread he ate [39:6]. However, trouble was again around the corner. Potiphar's wife began to lust after Joseph and proceeded to entice him. But Joseph was a true man of God and when things got to hot he did what many Christians today fail to do, he ran; right out of his clothes. She used his clothes to accuse and frame him of rape. Can you imagine doing all you know is right and somehow something always goes wrong? He was placed in jail and in spite of his suffering he did not forsake neither did he blame God.

Let me explain how God was involved though it may not appear He was. Understand that in those times what Joseph was accused of meant immediate death. Potiphar was captain of Pharaoh's army and a ruler of the time. Any infraction or betrayal meant certain death. Nevertheless, his life was spared and he became a prisoner of the king. Only an all powerful, all knowing God can intervene in such a way. When we think of prisons today, we picture clean facilities good food and plenty of exercise, which may be why some individuals frequent them so much. Joseph's prison, however, was dark, cold, and damp with bread and water as the main course. Criminals today might think twice about committing a crime if they had to deal with prison sentences like this.

Even in the midst of this, God was with Joseph [39:21], and he maintained the character of God in this damp, wet prison. He even earned the favor of the prison guard to the point that he was given charge of all the other prisoners [39:22]. In addition, while yet in prison God caused everything Joseph did to prosper. If we could only learn from Joseph's example, we would be better off. It's not enough to worship God in the good times, but we must worship him in the bad as well. Worship is not just what we do on Sunday morning. It's not just what we do at midweek service, but worship is how we live. Whatever we do that brings honor to God is worship [Purpose Driven Life]. No matter where we are, worship is being like Joseph who did not let his circumstances affect his position with God.

After some time Pharaoh's chief butler and baker offended him in such a manner that they were thrown in jail and put under Joseph's supervision. Something I find amazing is that the bible says Joseph served them [Gen 40:4].

How many of us would be willing to serve others in the midst of trial and tribulation. Most of us would be so busy with our own trouble that we would miss the opportunity to be a true example of the living God. He was even willing to interpret their dreams without hesitation, yet he acknowledged it was God who truly interprets. After listening he gave the butler and the baker the meaning of each one's dream. The butler was to be restored to his position, but the baker was to be killed. And in three days everything happened just as Joseph said it would. Except, the butler forgot about Joseph's request to remember him to Pharaoh.

It was two years later, when Pharaoh had a dream that none of his magicians could interpret, that the butler finally remembered Joseph. He told Pharaoh all that Joseph did for him and the baker, and Pharaoh sent for Joseph. What would we have done after waiting two years? Many of us would have been filled with ourselves and refused to help. Why should I help after you left me hear for two years, some of us would say. Again, Joseph, acknowledging God as the true interpreter, was willing to be a servant to the king [40:17]. His willingness to serve allowed

God to use him. And because he was able to fulfill Pharaoh's request, he was given the highest position in the land.

God had a plan for Joseph, and he has a plan for each of us. Even when it seems the bottom is falling out we must trust God. Romans 8:28 says, *"all things work together for good to them that love the Lord, and are called according to His purpose."* James 1:3-4 says, *"knowing this, that the trying of your faith produces patience. But let patience have her perfect work that ye may be perfect and entire wanting nothing."* We must understand suffering is for our benefit. Joseph would never have been the type of ruler God wanted if he had not endured suffering. God was preparing Joseph through those trials and He is preparing us when we are allowed to go through trials.

Everyone wants to achieve success the easy way. No one wants to experience pain or heartache, but the greatest achievements only come by these. Moreover, if you want to be great for God, then that is the only way it will come. Also, remember that in all you go through He will be with you all the way keeping you safe in His arms just as he did with Joseph. And in the midst of trials Joseph remained faithful to God, and the benefit of his faith was to become second in command in all Egypt and save his family and people from starvation.

Another great example is Paul. In 2Corinthians 11:23-27 he tells of his trials as he defends his apostleship. *"Are they ministering servants of Christ? I am talking as one beside himself, but I am more with far more extensive and abundant labors, with far more imprisonments, beaten with countless stripes, and frequently at the point of death. Five times I received from the hands of the Jews forty lashes all but one. Three times I have been beaten with rods, once I was stoned; three times I have been aboard a ship wrecked at sea, a whole night and a day I have spent adrift on the deep. Many times on journeys exposed to perils from rivers, perils of bandits, perils from my own nation, perils from the Gentiles, perils in the city, perils in the desert places, perils in the sea, perils from those posing as believers, but destitute of Christian knowledge and piety, In toil and hardship, watching often through sleepless nights, in hunger and thirst, frequently driven to fasting by want, in cold and exposure and lack of clothing.*" Many of us would look at all these circumstances and question, where is God? But Paul did not; he recognized it was part of being an apostle for Christ. And, in spite of all he endured, God kept him. He kept him physically. He did not allow Paul to die. God kept him spiritually. He did not allow Paul to fall from the faith. However, Paul could have chosen to turn away. In a sense, he had ever right to but did not. How many of us would choose to continue on if we had to endure what Paul endured? I believe Christians today, at least in America, are weak. When it comes to suffering for the sake of the gospel we don't have a clue. We falter under the most trivial of circumstances.

In 1Corinthians 10:13 Paul tells us "*He can be trusted not to let you be tempted and tried and assayed beyond your ability and strength of resistance and power to endure.*" If this is the case why do we fall? We fall because we do not really trust in Him whom we say we trust. If we trust Him He will keep us. Like Joseph, and like Paul God will keep us. Just as their lives were not without trials, yours and mine will not be without them either.

I can personally attest to God's keeping power. Although I am a minister, my full time vocation was once a truck driver and I never had an experience like the one I am about to share with you. I used to drive for a local company in the Atlanta Georgia area. I was traveling east on interstate 20 returning to the terminal from my last delivery. It was raining and, of course, the road was wet. As I approached an onramp, I noticed another tractor-trailer entering the highway. That would appear to be normal, but as this driver entered the highway, he was right next to me. Also quite normal, but the driver of this truck continued to move over into the lane I was in forcing me to slam on my brakes (remember the road is wet). When I did that the trailer I was pulling began to jackknife and I could feel the truck begin to flip over. Only God could do what happened next. I had lost control, but by the grace of God He straightened out the truck and got me off the road onto the shoulder. Another truck driver pulled over behind me to see if I was all right. After I said I was fine, just shaken up, he said, "I don't know how you straightened that thing out, I thought you were going to flip over." I was a new Christian at the time so I didn't say anything elaborate, but I new beyond a shadow of doubt that God kept me. I could have badmouthed the driver of that other truck, but I believe that God was proving His existence to me. He wanted me to know early in my Christian walk that He is a keeper. If I had focused on the other driver I might have missed what God was doing for me.

Not only does God keep us spiritually and physically, but mentally as well. Many people worry about Alzheimer's and other age related diseases that affect the mind, but God will keep your mind. Isaiah 26:3 states, *thou will keep him in perfect peace whose mind is stayed on thee. For God has not given us the spirit of fear, but of power and of love and of a **sound mind** [2Tim 1:7]. What does it mean to be in perfect peace? Perfect peace means perfect completeness (in number), safety, soundness (in body), welfare, health, prosperity, peace, quiet, tranquility, and contentment (Strongs). Having a sound mind means your mind is self-controlled, and moderate. It also means to be sound, to be well, to be in good health. In essence, free from flaw, defect, or decay as defined by Webster's. However, the key is our minds must be focused, fixed, concentrated on God.

Peter tells us in chapter 1 verse 5 of his first letter, we are being kept by God's power through our faith. The word kept which is from the root keep in Greek means to guard, or garrison. If you are in the military you will understand what this means. But for those of us who are not let me explain. Garrison is a verb that means to occupy with troops. Understand what God does, as he did for Joseph, Paul, and me, he keeps us by surrounding and occupying us with His troops. The heavenly army is sent to keep watch and guard against the enemy of our souls. And, not only do the troops go with us, at times He will send them before us [Ex 23:20]. Sometimes when we go through trials it is a test from God [Deut 8:3]. He wants to prove us [James 1:2-3] and make us into better people for the work of the kingdom and for the age to come.

Finally, we must live for today, we can't live tomorrow in today's blessing. Faith is about relying on God for today's needs [Ex 16:20]. He taught the disciples to pray, *"Give us this day our daily bread"* [Matt 6:11] and *"do not worry or be anxious about tomorrow, for tomorrow will have worries and anxieties of its own"* [Matt 6:34 Amp]. God promises to keep us day by day so let's have faith Him day by day.

Benefit 2

The second benefit of faith is God will heal you. Consequently, I have come to realize and understand that the healing we often ask for is not necessarily the healing we need. The word heal has three distinct definitions we need to know and understand. And, as we explore them maybe we can better decipher which of these we really need.

The first definition for heal is restore to health; many times because of doubt healing in any of the three forms does not take place. You must realize that you cannot use Christ's name effectively if you are not convinced of His power. However, if you recognize doubt and deal with it accordingly healing can still take place. In Mark 9:17-24 there is a story of a man struggling with this very thing. He was at the brink of despair, but he realized his condition. His son suffered since childhood with a demon that physically abused and tormented him. Can you imagine having to face such a challenge? He must have done everything he new to no avail. Even though the father did not suffer himself with this affliction, he was responsible for the well being of his son. Just as Jesus intercedes for us, as parents we are intercessors for our children.

This man seeing, for years, his son's torment was at a lost. But, he had come to the master. Jesus said to him, *"anything is possible to him who believes."* I stated earlier that the man realized his condition; it was a condition of doubt. In verse 24, it says the father cried out, but we must understand what this really means. The amplified says it this way, "at once the father of the boy gave an eager, piercing, inarticulate cry with tears." This was not simply crying, but was a groaning, screaming type of cry. It was a cry of distress and despair. And then these words, *"Lord I believe, help my unbelief!"* Sometimes life's situations can beat us down. And the longer we deal with them the more our faith begins to waiver, but all you and I have to do is recognize. Once we recognize and deal with our doubt God can work it out. Jesus healed the boy commanding the spirit never to enter him again.

Let us turn our attention to children for a moment, Mark 10:15 says unless we accept the kingdom as a child we will not enter it. Why as a child? Because a child's faith is true, strong, and unwavering. Every child believes dad is the strongest man in the world, and every child believes mom can heal a boo boo with her kiss. It's only as we grow older that our faith begins to change and everything needs to be proved. The older we get the more independent we want to be; so we don't think we need our parents anymore. Unfortunately, we treat God the same way. We get to a particular spiritual level and think we can be independent from God. However, God wants us to go back to that childlike faith as it relates to him.

Let me tell you a story. When I was a child I suffered from eczema, a disease attributed to very dry skin. I visited tons of doctors and dermatologists. I used all kinds of medicines and skin shampoos, but nothing worked. In spite of the dismal results I continued to believe that one-day I would be healed. I was plagued with this disease into my early twenties; however, as the years progressed there was a decrease in the amount of eczema that actually appeared on my skin. And today I can praise God, for it was neither doctor nor medicine, but the Healer Himself touched me and made me whole.

He tells us in Matthew 21:22 *"if you believe you shall receive"*, so why do we doubt God's ability. Do we not believe the word as we say? Doctors, psychologists, and sociologists have done studies for years on patients and faith. In these studies, it has been proven that people who held some form of faith were more likely to be healed than those without faith. And surprisingly enough, not all those who were healed were Christians. But because they had faith they were healed. Now my question is, if a non-Christian has faith enough to be healed why not God's redeemed? Some people may be asking right now, how do I know God wants to heal me? Scripture has the answer.

Paul pleads with God, in 2Cor 12:8-10, to heal him of an

infirmity. But, God tells him, *"My grace is sufficient."* Yes there will be sickness and disease; however, I believe according to scripture that whatever God's will is He will let you know. He will not leave you out in the cold. If He's the same yesterday, today, and forever why would he do that for Paul and not for you? It's only a matter of faith.

The second definition for heal is to cause an undesirable condition, or situation to be overcome. In chapter 15:18-19 of Jeremiah we find him suffering persecution. He is alone and feels the pain of one standing by himself for the principles of God. He feels pressure from the people and question God's faithfulness. Why is he questioning God's faithfulness? He is questioning because not only are the people pressuring him, but the king who is supposed to stand for God is also pressuring him [2Chron 36:12]. God tells Jeremiah, in essence, you need to turn from this doubt and if you do, then I will settle you. Sometimes we are left in situations or circumstances because we doubt God, but if we repent of our doubt God will settle us. He will take care of the situation if we ask and not doubt. Moreover, we must not ask just once, but we must ask continuously.

In Luke 18:1-8 Jesus tells the parable of a widow who continues to pester this judge. She continues to request his help for her situation, and because of her persistence he gives in to her request. Verse 8 is key to knowing and understanding the benefit of persistent prayer. Just because we don't get an answer immediately we want to toss God out the window. We tell ourselves that God is not listening and isn't going to help us with our problem. On the other hand, because we have been taught for so long to pray once and forget it, we pray once and forget it.

This parable, however, is a prime example of how we need to be persistent in our prayers continuing to go to God until the answer comes. He says in verse 7&8, comparing God to the judge, *"will not our just God defend, protect, and avenge his elect who cry to Him day and night."* Notice he says day and night, which means continually. *"Will he defer them and delay help on their behalf?"* he continues, *"I tell you He will defend, protect, and avenge them speedily."* Now, hopefully I've established that we should and must pray continually, the word speedily in this text should be translated as suddenly, or unexpectedly. There are times when God will answer quickly, but most times he answers according to His timetable not ours. However, when he does answer, at that moment speedily, suddenly, and unexpectedly we receive it.

Dottie Peebles wrote a song entitled, <u>On Time God</u>. In it she sang, "He may not come when you want Him, but He'll be there right on time He's an on time God Yes he is." Don't fret and don't give up when you're going through just keep the faith and keep praying; God will come through for you.

But that's not the end the latter part of verse 8 states,

"when the Son of Man comes will he find persistence in faith on the earth." It's important for us and to God that we are persistent in our faith not wavering, but standing firm. We ought to be steady not being tossed to and fro by every wind that blows. We ought to have a tight grip on the faith that saved us from sin keeping it close to our hearts. God is looking for those who are like this. Will you be among them when he returns? Will he be able to say, *"well done good and **faithful** servant?"* What undesirable conditions or situations are you going through? If you continue to stand in-spite of, you can hear

those words. Be like Jeremiah, though everyone may be against you, forget your doubt and do what God has ordained for you to do: stand firm and reap the benefits.

The third and final definition for heal is to restore to original purity or integrity. The bible says the gold has become dim the pure gold has changed. The precious sons of Zion once worth their weight in gold are merely esteemed as earthen vessels [Lam 4:1-2 states]. When Jeremiah says the most pure gold has changed he is not merely speaking of some precious metal he is speaking of the children of Israel. And not only is he speaking of them, but he is speaking of all mankind. God's most precious creation [man] has been damaged. In Ecc 7:29 Solomon writes, *God made man upright, however, they sought evil desires*. Man [humankind] was made pure, but that purity has been tainted and needs restoration. We are compared to gold because like gold we must go through a purification process.

Let's take an in-depth look at the process. In order for gold to be purified it must first suffer intense heat. This causes the impurities to rise to the surface enabling them to be scraped off. Understand this,

God puts us through the fire of trials to rid us of the impurities in our lives. Those things, which are not pleasing to Him, must be scraped off, and only by fire [trial] can this process take place [Job 23:10]. As Christians we should not be surprised when certain things happen just remember God is purifying you.

We are also compared to gold because of its character. Gold is ductile allowing it to be drawn out into tiny wires or threads without breaking. It is also malleable meaning it can be shaped or extended into extraordinarily thin sheets. For example, one ounce of gold can be hammered into a 100 square-foot sheet. Gold never reacts with oxygen (one of the most active elements), which means it will not rust or tarnish [goldinstitute.org].

How does this help us understand God purifying us? Like gold, God wants us to be ductile and malleable. He wants us to bend without breaking. He wants us to extend, or stretch beyond what we perceive our abilities are and accomplish great things for the Kingdom, in other words, He wants us to increase our faith. He wants us to remain pure and not be rusted or tarnished by sin. In order for these things to take place we must be purified.

Gold in its pure form is transparent: [Rev 21:18-21] one definition for transparent is, to be free from pretense or deceit. (If I weren't typing this right now I'd be jumping on my feet). God wants to rid us of every impure thought, word, or deed and it's not so much for us to be transparent to Him, but we need to be transparent to ourselves. He wants us to see who we really are, and it enables Him to know those who are His as we endure the process.

Why does God need to know His own? Again, it's not so much for Him, but for us, however, just as gold comes in many forms so do people. The character of pure gold has been discussed above, but there are many types. We will look at a few that are pretty similar in character as they relate to jewelry.

Gold filled jewelry is made of a thin outer layer of gold on top of a base metal. Gold plated jewelry is a metal with a thin layer of gold on the surface, also called electroplating [enchantedlearning.com]. Both of these pieces of jewelry are only layered in gold they are not pure. So when they come up against adversity some of the gold scrapes off. When that happens the true metal shines through. There are people in the church, or out of the church that claim to be true Christians. However, when they face adversity, their true character shines forth and let's God and everyone else no who they really are. Instead of responding with Christian principles, they respond with the flesh.

There is also gold stone, which is a shimmering quartz stone that ranges in color from yellow to red to light green to light brown. The shimmer is caused by tiny metallic particles (mica) within the stone (not gold). Fools gold, very famous, is a shiny metallic mineral (pyrite) that looks like gold, but is actually a form of

iron [enchantedlearning.com].
These two stones are not gold
at all they just look like gold.
Hence there are individuals
who look like Christians, but
are not even close. They wear
the right close and say the right
things at the right time around
the right people. But, when
they are with friends or family
they despise the name of Jesus
by their actions. So, in an effort
to weed these gold filled, gold
plated, gold stoned, gold fooled
individuals out and produce
pure Christians God sends us
all through the fire (trial).

God wants no substitutes
He wants the real thing not
diluted, mixed, or covered over.
He wants pure righteous vessels

fit for use in the Kingdom [1Pet 1:22]. So in order for us to become pure we must endure this process continually. Why continually, because we'll never truly reach perfection until Christ comes to redeem us from the earth, but we must be prepared now and this is how we prepare. In addition, it is our faith that ignites the fire and allows us to reap the benefit knowing God is working everything out for our good. This is where the armor of God comes into play. The armor also helps us withstand the fire of trial: above all the shield of faith [Eph 6:16]. Let's look at the armor for a few minutes.

First, we need to understand that during Paul's time, a soldier's armor was an important part of his life. A roman soldier put his armor on before he left home and he wore it daily even in peacetime. However, due to the times in which the Romans lived a soldier was required to wear his armor daily. As Christians we too should wear our spiritual armor daily and should dress before we leave home. And I feel we should not only wear it until we get home like the soldiers did, but I feel we should have it on at all times even while we are asleep, for the enemy is always at work and we must always be on guard.

Now let's look at the individual pieces of armor following the order listed in scripture beginning with the belt of truth. The belt used by Roman soldiers during Jesus' time had two purposes. It was used similarly to the belts we wear today to hold up, or keep tight our pants. The Roman armor was a series of loose fitting chains all linked together in length and width. It hung from his shoulders to just below the groin area. Because it was loose a belt was needed to keep it tight against the body. We know Satan is the father of lies and has been from the beginning. Knowing this, we need to keep truth close to us at all times so that the deceiver cannot deceive us.

Next we will look at the breastplate. This was an important piece of armor. The heart is the control center of life. The heart controls blood flow to every part of the body including, and especially to the brain. Even a minor problem with the heart can mean trouble. So, the breastplate was protection against blows and strikes to the chest with the sword. If the heart stops you die and the Romans knew the heart had to be protected. It is the same in the spirit. Without protecting the heart a believer is more susceptible to blows that could kill. The heart is the center of our physical life; Christ must be the center of our spiritual life. Without Christ at the center you die.

Having our feet shod; the soldier's footwear was almost as important as the breastplate. A Roman soldier had to be mobile. Most of their fighting was done in hand-to-hand combat. An enemy would approach from any direction and he had to move quickly. Their shoes were equivalent to athletic cleats with nails underneath. And, they were designed so they could go long distances in short times and over rough terrain. As

Christians we need to have firm footing. In other words, we cannot waiver back and forth. We must be sure in our faith and ready for battle. We must be mobile, agile, and flexible in motion when it comes to this spiritual battle. We must also endure the long road and rough terrain as we go through. If our foundation is not sure we fall.

Moving on to the helmet, we will bypass the shield for a moment, the Roman helmet was and is very different from our modern day helmets. It had a sloped edge down the back to protect the neck and two flaps that draped between the ears and eyes. It was important to protect the back of the neck in those days because it was a vulnerable area. An enemy would attempt to sneak up from behind and chop of an opponent's head. The flaps protected from side attacks. From the spiritual side we must remember that the battle for our salvation and souls is in the mind. Satan attacks our thoughts. He tries to get us to do things, say things, and ultimately turn from our faith. We must constantly renew our minds against his attacks. We must not lose our heads.

Now we get to the one weapon used to attack. The Roman sword was short and double-edged. As I stated earlier, they fought in hand-to-hand combat and their swords were designed for it. The size of the sword was not as important as the technique of the soldier wielding it. Roman soldiers were perfect in the field of combat and showed no mercy. The sword was used for offense and defense. Likewise, the word of God should be wielded wisely offensively and defensively. It should never be used on an ally, which is any believer regardless of denomination, only on the enemy. A roman soldier would never attack one of his own, but would come to the defense of his fellow soldier without hesitation. We must acknowledge, and participate in, the battle. A soldier cannot be afraid to fight, and he or she cannot fight without a weapon. A Christian without the word is like a soldier without his sword: helpless.

The next peace of armor is usually skipped over or left out completely. This is the armor of prayer. *And pray in the spirit on all occasions...* [Eph 6:18]. The Romans were ruthless, cruel and devoted to acts of violence. However, they were also very religious. They worshipped with all their hearts the many gods they had. Some gods were over other gods, and the soldiers would pray and sacrifice to them before going into battle. The Christian soldier should also pray. But, he should pray to the one and only true God and his son Jesus Christ. Even Jesus took time to pray to the father during his life on earth. The Romans prayed so their gods would help them. So, too, the Christian prays so that the God of heaven will assist him or her in battle. If the Romans saw the benefit of praying to gods that did not exist how much more of a benefit to the saints who pray to the living God?

Lastly, we come to the most important part of the armor. I saved this for last purposely. *Above all* *take up the shield of faith…* [Eph 6:16]. The Roman shield was rectangular and as tall as the soldier carrying it. He used it to advance while using his sword, or he would crouch behind it for protection against arrows and spears. The Roman soldiers soaked the shield in water until it was saturated. This made the shield heavy, yet it was beneficial in extinguishing flaming arrows being shot by the enemy. The Christian shield works the same; it is soaked in the blood of Jesus and is beneficial for extinguishing the flaming arrows the devil is shooting at you. Let me share something that may seem a little radical, but it's truth. None of the other pieces of armor is effective unless you have the shield of faith to accompany it.

Walk with me for a minute. Let's imagine you're dressing in armor, but all you have is the belt of truth. Truth is good, but truth without faith is ineffective. You're still susceptible to attacks by the enemy. However, truth accompanied with faith can help protect you. Next, you put on the breastplate of righteousness. With truth and righteousness, you assume everything is all right, but if not accompanied by faith the enemy causes you to retreat. Although, if faith accompanies these two you can advance on the enemy. Then you add your gospel boots. Now you have truth, righteousness, and the gospel of peace. However, without faith you are left open to the advancement of the enemy. With faith, these three can cover you from the enemy's tactics. Next, you add the helmet of salvation to your uniform. With salvation in the mix, you begin to make progress in your thinking, but this progress is limited and only has temporary effects on the enemy if faith is not in place. Now you grab your sword so you can strike the enemy, but he is able to elude you if you don't have faith. Finally, you begin to pray for God's assistance unfortunately you don't have faith, therefore, his ability to assist you is thwarted.

Hopefully, you understand the point I'm trying to make. If you put every piece, or every element of this spiritual armor on without the accompaniment of faith it will be useless. Faith (your shield) allows you to move forward on the enemy. It gives you the confidence to advance and enhances all the other pieces of armor making them more effective.

Benefit 3

This benefit is the last, but most important of the three. God will keep you and He will heal you, but all else plays second fiddle to His ultimate benefit, which is to save you. The bible tells us in Zephaniah 3:17 that *God is the one who saves*. This benefit supersedes all other benefits we obtain from God. He wants every man; women, boy, and girl to be saved and He will if you have faith in him to. Before we go any further let's discuss what salvation really is. In other words, what does it really mean to be saved? Romans 10:13 says, *whoever calls upon the name of the Lord will be saved*. What does that mean? We need to back up to verse 9.

First, we must acknowledge and confess him as Lord with our lips and then believe in our hearts that God raised him from the dead. Why must we confess first? Let me give you a true analogy. In my first real experience with Christianity in the Baptist church, I had to go through a class called catechism. Catechism means a summary of religious doctrine often in the form of questions and answers. The Deacon asked questions to the class that were related to what we could, or should believe as it related to the bible. He told the class that we needed to tell ourselves consistently that we believed. He explained that the more we told ourselves we believed the more we would actually believe. Therefore, it is important to confess with your mouth, not just once, but constantly so the heart will believe what the mouth is saying.

Jesus says, *"I am come that they might have life, and that they might have it more abundantly"*(John 10:10(KJV).

In order to understand what he means by this we must understand what abundantly actually means. The Greek definition for abundantly includes the word violently[4053]. This may seem strange and foreign to many of you, but when we look at the passage in light of this meaning, it changes our understanding. Now we understand that we have life, not just abundantly, but violently. Why violently? Because the scripture says, *from the days of John the Baptist until the present time the kingdom of heaven has endured violent assault and violent men seize it by force (as a precious prize-a share in the heavenly kingdom is sought with most ardent zeal and intense exertion)*(matt 11:12). Salvation is not for spectators. You cannot stand by and watch from the stands. This is a full contact sport and in order to gain the prize you must fight for it. And, you not only have to fight to get it you have to fight to keep it.

Now I know someone is thinking you don't have to do anything to receive salvation and that is true. However, how many of us Christians can honestly say we didn't battle with the decision. Does not Satan come against us at that point? Do we not waiver between the spirit's call and the enemies' call? Not only do we fight the enemy, but we fight against our flesh as well. So I hope you understand that even the very decision for salvation is a battle, which allows us to see that on all levels of spirituality we are at war. So let us be like an Olympic athlete who strives for the gold medal with ardent (fiery) zeal and intense (extreme) exertion. In other words, let us focus all of our might, strength, power, and ability in accomplishing our goal.

In spite of all this, let us keep in mind that it is because of Christ's sacrifice that we even have the opportunity to fight for salvation. He died to save us. Let's look at this word for a moment. To save means: to deliver, protect, heal, preserve, do well, be(make) whole[4982]. As we look at this, keep in mind the battle. Also, I am dealing here with salvation of the soul exclusively maybe God will allow me to get deeper in another book or at a later time in some way. Salvation includes deliverance, which means to rescue or save from someone or something, to be set free[web]. To be saved means to be set free from sin. We all, at one time or another, were bound to sin, but Christ died to free us from the bonds of sin. It's like being in prison all your life and having someone finally free you. Remember the Israelites went through this very thing. There were some that had never known what it was like to be free. Can you imagine what it was like when they finally made it across the red see, what a feeling?

Salvation also includes protection, which means to cover or shield from exposure, injury, or destruction[web]. God will shield you from the exposure to sin. Not that you won't be exposed, but he will be the sun block that shields you from the harmful rays of the sun so that you will not be injured by the cancerous rays that can destroy your skin cells.

In other words, He will allow you to live in a sinful world without being sinful yourself. You will be exposed to all the dangers, all the hurts, and all the sorrows, but you will not be harmed by them and you will be saved from the impending destruction to come.

Healing is part of salvation as well. If you are not saved then your soul is sick and needs healing. Only through the blood of Jesus can your soul be healed. Medicine can't do it vitamins can't do it even natural herbs, which are in great demand these days can't do it. We must put our faith and trust in Jesus Christ by confessing and believing. And

remember, don't just confess
once but continue to confess
over and over so that you will
be convinced in what you
believe.